W9-AKB-006

Sneed B. Collard III
BEAKS!

Illustrated by **Robin Brickman**

ini Charlesbridge

For Deb Clow, one of my favorite beak-watchers.

— Much love, Sneed

For all of the wonderful children at the

Williamstown Elementary School,

and Susan Hyde, the librarian.

— R. B.

Published by Charlesbridge Publishing
85 Main Street, Watertown, MA 02472
(617) 926-0329
www.charlesbridge.com

Library of Congress Cataloging-in-Publication Data
Collard III, Sneed B.
    Beaks / by Sneed B. Collard III; illustrated by Robin Brickman.
    p. cm.
Summary: Simple text describes various bird beaks and how birds use them to eat, hunt, and gather
food. Includes a quiz.
    ISBN 1-57091-387-0 (reinforced for library use)
    ISBN 1-57091-388-9 (softcover)
    1. Bill (Anatomy)—Juvenile literature. [1. Bill (Anatomy) 2. Birds.] I. Brickman, Robin, ill. II.
Title.
QL 697 .C66 2002
573.3'5518—dc21   2001004362
(hc) 10 9 8 7 6 5 4 3 2
(sc) 10 9 8 7 6 5 4 3 2

The three-dimensional illustrations in this book were made of paper painted
and sculpted by Robin Brickman.
The display type and text type were set in Monotype Dante.
Designed by Susan Mallory Sherman
The art was photographed by Gamma One.
Color separations were made by Ocean Graphic Company Ltd.
Printed and bound in China by Everbest Printing Co. Ltd through
Four Colour Imports Ltd., Louisville, Kentucky
Production supervision by Brian G. Walker

Birds have no teeth.
No hands. No antlers, horns,
or spines. But birds have beaks.
And beaks are enough.

Woodpecker Finch

Birds use beaks to get food.
But not all beaks work the same.

Small beaks peck.

Song Sparrows

Sparrows hop along like little kangaroos, pecking at things that look tasty. Their favorite food is dry seeds. When they find a seed, the sparrows use their short, cone-shaped beaks to crack the husk and swallow the seed. Sparrows can move their upper and lower bills from side to side. This helps them handle even tiny seeds without dropping them.

Heavy beaks crush.

Macaws

Like sparrows, many macaws eat seeds. Unlike sparrows, macaws eat very big seeds. With its heavy, sharp beak, the scarlet macaw cuts through the fleshy green fruit of an Indian almond tree. When the macaw reaches the hard nut, it crushes it and gulps down the nutritious seed inside. With such powerful beaks, macaws are able to dine on seeds that other rain forest birds can only dream about.

Long beaks probe.

Hummingbirds

Long, thin bills help hummingbirds reach the energy-rich nectar they need to survive. Different bills fit different shapes of flowers. The white-tipped sicklebill hummingbird inserts its long, curved bill into the opening of the Heliconia flower. With its long, tubelike tongue, the bird drinks up the Heliconia's sweet syrup and then zooms away to the next flower.

Hooked beaks tear.

Eagles

Eagles and other birds of prey are hunters, and their beaks are designed to help them eat flesh. Bald eagles feed mostly on fish. They fly low over a lake or stream and snatch their prey with their long talons. An eagle takes its fish to a perch or nest. Then the bird uses its sharp, hooked beak to strip away the fish's scaly skin and pick the meat off its bones.

Beaks are made light.

Toucans

A toucan's large, colorful beak looks heavy, but it is built like a honeycomb and is almost as light as a feather. The toucan uses this long, light tool to pluck berries and insects from tree branches. The beak also allows toucans to identify each other. Unfortunately, a light beak is easily damaged. Toucans sometimes break off pieces of their beaks while hunting or driving away other birds from a favorite fruit tree.

Or sturdy and strong.

Woodpeckers

Woodpeckers use their sturdy, pointed beaks to pound, drill, and tear into wood as they search for insects. Some, such as the acorn woodpecker, chip away holes where they store acorns and seeds. Fortunately, a woodpecker's skull is reinforced with extra-thick bone. This keeps the bird from getting brain damage while it is "woodpecking" away.

Beaks are even made upside down!

Flamingos

A flamingo's beak looks ridiculous—until you see how the flamingo eats. Flamingos feed with their heads upside down. Standing in shallow lakes and marshes, they draw water through their beaks by using their muscular tongues as pumps. Special strainers in the beak filter out the tiny plants and animals that the flamingo eats. Pigments in these foods give flamingos their bright, dizzying colors.

A skimming beak.

Skimmers

Like the flamingo's beak, a skimmer's beak looks like an accident. The bottom bill is longer than the top. The skimmer puts its backward beak to good use. To hunt, the bird flies with its lower bill slicing below the water's surface. When it strikes a fish, the bird snaps its beak shut, trapping the fish in a scissorslike grip. In this way, skimmers can catch fish without even getting wet.

A swishing beak.

Spoonbills

Spoonbills have flat, paddle-shaped beaks. To find food, spoonbills wade into shallow water and swish their open beaks back and forth. At the same time, the birds use their feet to stir up mud and the animals in it. Like skimmers, they hunt by touch, snapping their beaks closed on insects, fish, and other prey. Hunting in groups probably helps spoonbills stir up more food than hunting alone.

A stabbing beak.

Herons

A heron also wades, but it hunts differently than a spoonbill. A heron walks slowly through the shallows, pausing frequently to study the water. When it sees a fish or other animal, the heron quickly stabs its beak into the water and seizes its prey between its bills. Herons are strong birds and can catch and swallow surprisingly large fish and other animals.

A plunging beak.

Pelicans

A pelican fishing is one of nature's most thrilling spectacles. When a pelican spots a fish, the bird folds its wings and dives straight down at speeds of up to forty miles per hour. As the pelican crashes openmouthed into the water, the pouch on its lower bill puffs out to net its prey. After the water drains from the pouch, the pelican swallows its meal—but only if a sneaky seagull doesn't steal it first!

A prying beak.

Crossbills

A crossbill looks like it would starve to death with its screwball beak. However, the crossed tips of its beak allow the bird to pry apart the scales of pinecones and other cones. This exposes the cones' seeds, which the crossbill laps up with its sticky tongue. Despite their strange beaks, crossbills also eat fruit, insects, and the seeds of other plants.

Of course, beaks do more than get food. Beaks can show off.

Hornbills

Like toucans, hornbills grow large, brightly colored bills.
The bills of many hornbills are topped by a special
structure called a casque. Biologists believe that the
casque helps hornbills attract mates or identify the age
and sex of other hornbills. A hornbill's casque may also
amplify the bird's calls and help in knocking down fruit
and fighting off enemies.

Or build.

Bowerbirds

Many birds build nests, but male bowerbirds also build elaborate courts, or bowers, up to six feet tall. The birds construct the bowers with sticks and often decorate them with brightly colored objects. The bower's only purpose is to attract females to mate with. Once the male has mated, he takes no part in nest building. The female flies off to build a nest and raise the young all on her own.

Or dig.

Bee-eaters

From their name, it's not hard to guess that bee-eaters use their long, thin beaks to catch bees. Once it captures a bee, the bee-eater whacks it against a hard surface to knock off the bee's stinger and squeeze out its venom. The bird also uses its bill to dig a home. Bee-eaters nest in large colonies, where they dig burrows into dirt cliffs or the ground. These burrows provide shelter and safe places to raise the bee-eaters' young.

Beaks can change colors.

Western Gulls

The beaks of many birds change colors as they grow older. Seagull beaks are good examples. They go through several color combinations during the birds' first two or three years of life. Afterward, the bills continue to change colors between seasons. These changing colors probably help gulls recognize each other. They also give bird-watchers headaches as they try to identify birds such as this Western gull.

Or, once a year, get shed.

Puffins

Puffins are handsome birds that dive underwater to catch small fish in northern seas. The puffin's beak can hold up to two dozen herring at one time, but it is remarkable for another reason. Each breeding season, male puffins grow special, vividly colored sheaths around their beaks. These sheaths help the males show off and attract females. When mating season ends, the puffins shed their bright decorations until the following year.

Over time, beaks change.
And change again...

Hawaiian Honeycreepers

Over time, all life changes. We call this process
evolution. Often, one kind of plant or animal evolves
into many different forms. Scientists believe that all
Hawaiian honeycreepers evolved from a single kind
of finch that flew to Hawaii thousands of years ago.
Over time, the original finch evolved into more than
forty different forms or species. About half of these
species have become extinct, but twenty different
kinds of honeycreepers still live in Hawaii. As you
can see, their different beaks allow them to survive in
many different ways.

Including the beaks we see today.

Like all other living things, birds and their beaks continue to change as time flies forward. Some of the beaks we see today will survive into the future. Others will disappear or be replaced by new beaks that will allow the birds of tomorrow to survive better. This weeding out and replacement process is called natural selection. It's part of how plants and animals evolve or change over time, and it's what has given us the wonderful world—and wonderful beaks—we have today.

Bittern

Test your "beak-ability"

Peregrine Falcon

By now you should know that a beak's major purpose is to get food. On this page are six different birds and their beaks. Just for fun, study each bird and ask yourself:

What would I eat with this beak?

Would I eat meat?

Roadrunner

Seeds?

Marbled Godwit

Fruit?

Cardinal

Insects?

Warbler

Plants?

Wood Duck

Look on page 32 for answers.

Books

To learn how to identify and watch birds, the following books are a good place to start:

Backyard Birds (Peterson Field Guides for Young Naturalists) by Jonathan P. Latimer and Karen Stray Nolting. Boston: Houghton Mifflin, 1999.

Birds of Prey (Peterson Field Guides for Young Naturalists) by Jonathan P. Latimer and Karen Stray Nolting. Boston: Houghton Mifflin, 1999.

Songbirds (Peterson Field Guides for Young Naturalists) by Jonathan P. Latimer and Karen Stray Nolting. Boston: Houghton Mifflin, 2000.

Other fun, informative books on birds include:

Birds of Prey: A Look at Daytime Raptors by Sneed B. Collard III. New York: Franklin Watts, 1999.

The Bald Eagle Returns by Dorothy Hinshaw Patent. Boston: Houghton Mifflin, 2000.

Web sites

Several excellent Web sites about birds can be found on the Internet:

www.birds.cornell.edu
The Web site for Cornell University Lab of Ornithology, containing a wealth of information about birds and scientific research on them.

www.peregrinefund.org
The Web site of the Peregrine Fund, an organization dedicated to saving endangered birds of prey.

www.audubon.org
A fun Web site of the Audubon Society, containing interesting bird facts and activities.

www.hawkwatch.org
The fascinating site of Hawkwatch, a group focusing on the migration and conservation of birds of prey.

Roadrunner

Answers:
Peregrine falcons eat mostly other birds.
Roadrunners eat reptiles, birds, insects, and small mammals.
Marbled godwits hunt and eat aquatic invertebrates that they find down in the sand.
Mallard ducks mostly eat plant matter, though sometimes they will eat a few insects.
Cardinals eat seeds and fruit.
Warblers eat mostly insects and occasionally some fruit.